Caring
For the School Year
Messages

40 Weeks of
Daily Discussion Ideas
on Character

SHARON L. BANAS

For information, please contact:

The Education People, Inc.
334 Underhill Ave., #4C & 4D
Yorktown Heights, NY 10598

(800) 624-1634
Tel (914) 455-2400
Fax (914) 455-2271

Project Management Doug Gibson
Cover design by Sandy Nordman
Interior/text design by Sara Sanders, SHS Design

2nd Printing, 2003

ISBN 1-892056-12-7
$14.95

Quantity Purchases
Schools, professional groups, clubs and other organizations may qualify for special terms when ordering quantities of this title. For ordering information, contact the Customer Service Department of Character Development Publishing at the numbers listed above.

Introduction

This book contains caring messages for forty weeks, with a quote or idea that interprets the message for each day of the week. The weeks were not dated because of differences in school calendars. You'll have shorter school weeks when five messages are not needed, but you can adapt those pages. Certain messages may also seem more appropriate for certain times of the year, so the weeks do not have to be used consecutively. For example, I would use the weekly message "Count Your Blessings!" the week before Thanksgiving, or the message "Nurture Our Environment!" during the week in April when we celebrate Earth Day.

Other weeks you may choose to develop a community theme or respond to a news event of great importance. For example, in some districts the third week of October is set aside to encourage students not to use drugs. I have enclosed a sample in Supplement 1 to illustrate how we incorporated "Drug Free Week" into our scheduled messages.

As part of our efforts in character education I also believe we should teach our children about national holidays and important historical events. You'll find descriptions of them at the back of this book, and I encourage you to use them in addition to the weekly messages. I began doing this when I became aware that many of our children do not have a clear understanding of the meaning of these holidays. Please add any other celebrations or events that you feel are acceptable and important in your school community.

At Sweet Home Middle School, where I have been privileged to teach for almost thirty years, we use the daily message after the morning announcements. It becomes more meaningful if you can have the adult or students making the announcements add some personal examples or interpretations of the message. For example, if the message is about caring perhaps they could mention a person who works in the building, such as a custodian, who always demonstrates a caring attitude toward others.

Several years ago, our PTA provided an electronic message board for our school cafetorium. This became a place where we could remind students of the caring message during lunch. We're located on a busy road, and we also have a large sign in front of our school where we place our weekly message. It's a way to reach out to the community. We've received many positive comments about the messages. Perhaps you could also encourage other community groups to use the message in their workplaces or at their meetings. We give a school planner to all of our students, and we have the messages printed in our new planners.

The message can also be sent in advance to district offices or to the transportation department. Some of our bus drivers have spoken with the students about the messages and posted them on their buses. Students have told me that their parents discuss the message at home. One child told me it is often one of the topics discussed at their dinner table. They share stories, discuss goals that pertain to the message, or talk about ways they can fulfill the message in their own lives.

There are also ways that the messages can be integrated and infused into the classroom. If there is a short homeroom period, or an advisor/advisee period, this could be the ideal place for a discussion about the message. I am a storyteller, and I have found that students love to hear personal anecdotes from adults (especially those about our mistakes or how we struggled before succeeding). For example, if the message is about setting goals, you can share a personal goal. If it is about overcoming obstacles, you can share a story about yourself or someone you know who overcame a difficulty.

We also use a great deal of paper in schools. Encourage teachers to include the message or an interpretation of it at the bottom of a worksheet or test. Administrators can also use the messages in their memos. A former principal of our school often used the message to remind the faculty and staff about our responsibilities. One week when the message was about "Respect," he reminded us that we could show more respect for each other if we remembered to send out field trip notices two weeks in advance. I would also encourage colleagues to stuff mailboxes with additional quotes or stories that pertain to the messages. I even receive them from parents and students.

Teachers of English Language Arts can use these thoughts for writing assignments. Students can be asked to write an interpretation of the message or to apply it to a story. Perhaps some of the students could share these stories if they choose to do so. Some character educators have students keep "character journals," and this would be an ideal place to use the message. Stories could also be read that are related to the theme for the week.

Of course, these are just a few suggestions and I hope that you will have many other uses for the messages. I wish you the best of luck in all of your character education efforts—it really makes a difference.

Sharon L. Banas

Part I:
Weekly Messages

CARING MESSAGE FOR WEEK 1:

Realize your own potential!

MONDAY:

Welcome to a brand new school year! Think of it as the beginning of an adventure. Many opportunities will be offered to you—be ready to take advantage of them. Work hard, have fun, and keep your eyes and ears open to all of the activities, clubs, and teams you can join this year.

TUESDAY:

No two people in our school are exactly alike—we are all individuals! Each one of us has some special talents, and we want you to use your talents to make a difference in our school.

WEDNESDAY:

If you want to be your own person you must be willing to think for yourself. Everyone makes mistakes, and you may make some wrong decisions, but you will gain courage and self-confidence by making your own choices.

THURSDAY:

Don't let others put you down. All of us possess wonderful qualities we may not yet have discovered. Focus on what's great about you, and let someone's negative comment slide off your back.

FRIDAY:

This weekend, think about some goals you'd like to accomplish this year. There is a saying, "If we don't have goals we don't know where we might be headed." Each of us needs a plan for success, or we won't know when we get there!

CARING MESSAGE FOR WEEK 2:

Strive for quality in everything you do!

MONDAY:

Hard work helps us realize our potential. If we strive for quality, our successes will bring us more confidence, and our confidence will bring us more success.

TUESDAY:

When you write your name on the top of your papers think about how those papers are a reflection of you. What impression do you give others by the way you do that small thing? Always do your best work and leave a good impression!

WEDNESDAY:

Promise yourself you'll do quality work. It will become a habit—and we know how hard it is to break a habit! If you form good habits now, it will lead to success in school—and success in other areas of life.

THURSDAY:

The difference between being ordinary and extraordinary is a little "extra" effort—so give the world your best try!

FRIDAY:

Discuss this Japanese proverb: "The reputation of a thousand years may be determined by the conduct of one hour."

CARING MESSAGE FOR WEEK 3:

Be responsible for your own actions!

MONDAY:

Being responsible means being accountable—admitting your mistakes or wrong actions and accepting the consequences for them. It also means doing without being told what you know you should do.

TUESDAY:

Even a woodpecker has to use his head in order to achieve success. Think carefully about consequences before you decide to act.

WEDNESDAY:

Abraham Lincoln said, "You can't escape the responsibility of tomorrow by evading it today."

THURSDAY:

Aristotle, the great Greek philosopher, said, "No one who desires to become good will become good unless he does good things." He advised his followers to ask themselves often: "Did I know that this was the right or wrong thing to do?"

FRIDAY:

When we do something wrong, we are often quick to think of excuses or quick to blame someone else. "It's not my fault!" is not something a responsible person says.

CARING MESSAGE FOR WEEK 4:

Have the courage to do the right thing!

MONDAY:

We all have a built-in warning system that is called a conscience. It tells us when something is wrong and it can keep us from doing the wrong thing. Don't be upset when your conscience bothers you—that's just the warning bell!

TUESDAY:

The best gift we can give others is our good example. When someone mentions a role model, you may think about a parent, teacher, or other adult. But each one of us is a role model for others every day. Try to be a good one.

WEDNESDAY:

Don't be afraid to try new things. We can amaze ourselves when we do something we didn't think we could accomplish. What a great feeling! Don't sell yourself short; be willing to take the risk.

THURSDAY:

A hero is simply a person who always tries to do his best, even if he makes a mistake. Sometimes it takes great courage to admit our mistakes and to say we are sorry. Be a hero today!

FRIDAY:

Your parents and teachers have taught you what it means to be good, and your conscience leads you in the right direction, but it's up to you to choose to do the right thing. What kind of person will you choose to be?

Friendship is a responsibility!

MONDAY:

10-25-18 Ralph Waldo Emerson, the great American writer and poet, said, "The only way to have a friend is to be one."

TUESDAY:

10-26-18 A true friend is a person who knows all of your faults and loves you anyway. Make your friends happy today simply by spending time with them—and don't point out their mistakes. Accept them for who they are! You can always feel comfortable with a friend.

WEDNESDAY:

If you are very lucky, you can have more than one best friend at the same time. Don't be too quick to leave someone out simply because you are with another person. When it comes to friendship, "The more the merrier."

THURSDAY:

10/31/18 A true friend is someone who makes us happy simply by being in his or her presence. If you have a friend who has a problem, just your being there will be a help. Sometimes we worry too much about not knowing the right thing to say when someone is hurting. Just be there to listen.

FRIDAY:

"If you can make me laugh, make me cry, make me mad, and cheer me up...then you are a friend."

—Unknown

CARING MESSAGE FOR WEEK 6:

Be proud of your country, your school and yourself!

MONDAY:

"Keep away from people who try to belittle your ambitions. Small people always do that, but the really great make you feel that you, too, can become great."

—*Mark Twain*

TUESDAY:

Be proud to be an American and be glad that we live in a country where we can make choices and express our opinions. If you see a problem in your community, take action by writing letters to important officials or attending town meetings.

WEDNESDAY:

If you want to feel a sense of pride in yourself, do something to help another person. Nothing will make you feel better about yourself!

THURSDAY:

"We must learn to live together as brothers or we will perish together like fools."

—*Dr. Martin Luther King Jr.*

FRIDAY:

Show your school spirit and take an active part in making our school a better place by volunteering your services. If you'd like to join a club or volunteer to be a student representative on a building committee, see your teachers or guidance counselor for suggestions.

CARING MESSAGE FOR WEEK 7:

Love, respect, and enjoy other people!

MONDAY:

"The only people you should try to get even with are those who have helped you." The author of that comment is unknown, but his idea is a challenge to us to care for each other.

TUESDAY:

If you witness an act of disrespect toward another person, don't be silent! You have an obligation to ask the disrespectful person to stop, or to tell an adult. It will make you feel better about yourself.

WEDNESDAY:

You can become a better, more caring person if you begin to show respect for everyone, even those who can't do anything special for you.

THURSDAY:

Abraham Lincoln said, "Most people are about as happy as they make up their minds to be." Find ways to enjoy the people around you!

FRIDAY:

A sense of humor is important. Be the kind of person who can laugh at yourself if you make a silly mistake. Studies have proven that laughter can be a very strong medicine and actually makes people healthier.

Improve your attitude!

MONDAY:

Attitude is actually a choice. It is our most important choice because it affects the way we live every single day.

TUESDAY:

"The race doesn't always go to the strongest or fastest. The one who wins the race is the one who thinks he can."

—*Unknown*

WEDNESDAY:

The great English writer Rudyard Kipling once said, "We have forty million reasons for failure, but not a single excuse."

THURSDAY:

A positive attitude requires a serious commitment. You can't control everything that happens to you, but you can choose what you feel and do. It is not easy to be positive, but we all like to be with positive people.

FRIDAY:

Instead of concentrating on what life brings to you, concentrate on the attitude you bring to life.

CARING MESSAGE FOR WEEK 9:

Learning means keeping your mind open!

MONDAY:

A member of the Seneca nation once said, "No one ever became wise by chance."

TUESDAY:

"Anyone who stops learning is old, whether at twenty or eighty."
—*Henry Ford*

WEDNESDAY:

Real learning is not a passive activity; it involves action. The great Greek philosopher Aristotle said, "What we have to learn to do, we learn by doing!"

THURSDAY:

Sophocles was an ancient Greek writer of tragedies. He reminded us that learning is a lifelong process when he said, "A man, though wise, should never be ashamed of learning more."

FRIDAY:

"It's what you learn after you know it all that counts."
—*Harry S. Truman, 33rd U.S. President*

CARING MESSAGE FOR WEEK 10:

Life is not always easy!

MONDAY:

Life is not always what we expect it to be nor what we want it to be. It doesn't help anything to complain and whine. Life is made better by working hard and reaching out to others for support. It doesn't mean we won't suffer, but we must learn to accept the challenge.

TUESDAY:

"A diamond is a chunk of coal made good under pressure." This unknown author meant that we become stronger when we work through our difficulties, and don't blame them on something or someone else.

WEDNESDAY:

Benjamin Franklin said, "Those things that hurt, instruct." He meant that we often learn the most valuable lessons of life when we are suffering and working through difficult times. When we overcome an obstacle we gain a tremendous sense of achievement.

THURSDAY:

"Character cannot be developed in ease and quiet. Only through the experience of trial and suffering can the soul be strengthened, vision cleared, ambition inspired, and success achieved."

—Helen Keller

FRIDAY:

"The ultimate measure of a man is not where he stands in a moment of comfort and convenience, but where he stands at times of challenge and controversy."

—Dr. Martin Luther King Jr.

CARING MESSAGE FOR WEEK 11:

Be an honest person!

MONDAY:

"If you tell the truth, you don't have to remember anything!"

—*Mark Twain*

TUESDAY:

Being honest is a struggle every day. It means doing all your work yourself; following rules even if no one is watching; and telling the truth about your age even if it means paying more for a ticket. Being honest takes effort, but it's always worth it because we can never fool ourselves.

WEDNESDAY:

Have you or one of your friends ever been the victim of a rumor? How did it make you or your friend feel? It's easy to stop a rumor that you hear about someone else—just refuse to pass it on.

THURSDAY:

"The greatest way to live with honor in the world is to be what you pretend to be."

—*Socrates*

FRIDAY:

Albert Einstein's advice about truth was: "One must not conceal any part of what one has recognized to be true." In other words, we need to tell the whole truth.

Count your blessings!

MONDAY:

It is easy for us to complain about things we do not have. Instead, let's be grateful for our many gifts and be willing to share them with others.

TUESDAY:

An anonymous author said, "It is better to light a candle than to curse the darkness." This means that, in time of trouble, it is better to get up and do something with what you have available.

WEDNESDAY:

There are so many reasons to give thanks. Make a list of all of the things and people who make a difference in your life and find a way to show your thanks this week.

THURSDAY:

True happiness can only be found when we learn to be content with what we have.

FRIDAY:

Being grateful will give you a sense of peace and will make others glad to be around you.

CARING MESSAGE FOR WEEK 13:

Do a good deed without being asked!

MONDAY:

If you notice something that needs to be done, take the initiative to do it. Pick up papers from the floor; pass out books; get someone a napkin or something to drink; dry the dishes; turn down the music if someone is on the phone—these are simple acts of kindness that will be appreciated by others.

TUESDAY:

William Wordsworth, a famous English poet, said, "The best portion of a good man's life are his little, nameless, unmentioned acts of kindness and love."

WEDNESDAY:

The great American poet Ralph Waldo Emerson said, "It is one of the greatest compensations of this life that no man can sincerely try to help another without helping himself." When we do something for another person it makes us feel good about ourselves.

THURSDAY:

At times we may regret the fact that we do not have enough money to buy someone we love a gift or take them somewhere special. However, doing small acts of kindness to make their life a little easier is a much better gift.

FRIDAY:

"Everybody can be great because we can serve. You don't have to have a college degree to serve. You don't have to make your subject and verb agree to serve. You only need a heart full of grace. A soul generated by love."

—*Dr. Martin Luther King Jr.*

CARING MESSAGE FOR WEEK 14:

Practice conscious acts of kindness!

MONDAY:

One of the greatest acts of kindness we can give to others is simply to show them that we are genuinely interested in them.

TUESDAY:

We seem to live in a world of "put downs"—TV characters, for example, seem witty because of their snappy insults. But real people are hurt by this kind of language. Try some kind words and notice the difference in people's reactions.

WEDNESDAY:

If you can do something kind for another person, don't wait until it's too late. It may really make a difference to the person, and you'll be glad you didn't miss the chance to do it.

THURSDAY:

Aesop, a Greek slave and author of our greatest fables, said, "No act of kindness, no matter how small, is ever wasted."

FRIDAY:

When someone is having a problem or feeling low, express your feelings of sympathy and say no more. Listen to him or her, or sit together in silence. Sometimes the kindest words are those not spoken at all.

CARING MESSAGE FOR WEEK 15:

Peace is a way of life!

MONDAY:

People often say they want peace in the world, but they don't take action to bring peace into their daily lives. Peace and a spirit of harmony begin inside each individual.

TUESDAY:

If you and a friend are arguing, then you both have a problem. The solution will come only if both of you are willing to listen to each other and compromise. You both will benefit from the results.

WEDNESDAY:

When we're having a serious disagreement with someone, we sometimes need to get help from others who are not involved in the situation. If you or someone you know is having a problem, remember you can get help by stopping in the guidance office, using peer mediation, or seeing one of your teachers or administrators.

THURSDAY:

"If we were supposed to talk more than we listen, we would have two mouths and one ear."

—*Mark Twain*

FRIDAY:

Mother Theresa lived as a peacemaker. She said, "When we say no to violence, we always imagine a knife, a bomb, a gun. However, to me, violence is caused by our attitude. For example, telling someone that they are good for nothing...If you and I will make that strong resolution to say "no" to violence and "yes" to peace by our kindness, by our attitude towards each other...it would help more than anything!"

Gordon

35

CARING MESSAGE FOR WEEK 16:

Stand up for what you know is right!

MONDAY:

Practicing justice means being careful that our actions don't harm others in any way. It also means not being too quick to criticize others, even if we find their actions annoying.

TUESDAY:

"Justice can not be for one side alone, it must be for both."

—*Eleanor Roosevelt*

WEDNESDAY:

When we practice justice, we get in the habit of doing our duties and performing at our best no matter how we feel. If you are having a terrible day, don't take it out on others.

THURSDAY:

Abraham Lincoln said, "The possibility that we may fail in the struggle ought not to stop us from supporting a cause we believe to be just." It is a good thing he was not afraid to fail.

FRIDAY:

The famous anthropologist, Margaret Mead, said, "Never doubt that a small group of thoughtful, committed citizens can change the world. Indeed, it is the only thing that ever has." History is full of stories about individuals who have made a big difference in the lives of others.

CARING MESSAGE FOR WEEK 17:

There is always time for courtesy!

MONDAY:

Always send a thank-you note or card when someone has given you a gift or done something especially thoughtful for you. These are always appreciated. If you owe someone a thank-you note, why not send it today?

TUESDAY:

Everyone likes to be spoken to politely. George Bernard Shaw, the famous playwright, said, "Without good manners human society becomes intolerable and impossible." Try to speak courteously to everyone, especially to people you don't know.

WEDNESDAY:

A true sign of good manners or courtesy is being nice to someone who is rude. It is a difficult task but also a powerful example for others.

THURSDAY:

When you are entering a building or a room, hold the door open for the person directly behind you. Good manners are infectious, and you'll influence others to be courteous.

FRIDAY:

"Nothing is more reasonable and cheap than good manners."

—Unknown

CARING MESSAGE FOR WEEK 18:

Use your time wisely!

MONDAY:

The only real preparation for tomorrow is what we do today, so let's not waste our chances by always wishing for tomorrow.

TUESDAY:

There is an old English proverb: "One of these days is none of these days." Don't put off until tomorrow something you should do today.

WEDNESDAY:

Remember the story of the tortoise and the hare. In this Aesop fable we are reminded that, "Slow and steady wins the race."

THURSDAY:

"Time is the coin of life. It is the only coin you have, and only you can determine how it will be spent. Be careful lest you let other people spend it for you."

—*Carl Sandburg*

FRIDAY:

In *Poor Richard's Almanack*, Benjamin Franklin wrote:
"Dost thou love life? Then do not squander Time; for that's the Stuff Life is made of."

Be content with what you have!

MONDAY:

No one enjoys being around complainers! Life isn't perfect for anyone. If you choose to be cheerful, others will be driven to you because of your positive attitude. Try to see the glass half full instead of half empty!

TUESDAY:

Benjamin Franklin said, "We never appreciate the value of water until the well has run dry." It's easy to take people, things, and even our freedom for granted. Try to remember to be thankful and to express your thanks to others.

WEDNESDAY:

The grass only seems greener on the other side. Contentment isn't getting what we want, but being satisfied with what we have.

THURSDAY:

People who are content learn to spend quiet time by themselves. It is a great stress reliever to reflect upon your actions and think about important decisions.

FRIDAY:

"When the door of happiness closes another opens, but often we look so long at the closed door that we do not see the one which has been opened for us."

—Helen Keller

Excellence is a habit!

MONDAY:

Excellence takes practice. Arthur Rubinstein once said the following about practicing his music:

> "If I miss one day, I notice it.
> If I miss two days, my friends notice it.
> If I miss three days, the public notices it."

TUESDAY:

Before you hand in any assignment, ask yourself if you have given it your best effort.

WEDNESDAY:

"We are what we repeatedly do. Excellence is, then, not an act, but a *habit.*"
                                                                        —*Aristotle*

THURSDAY:

Getting rid of old habits and forming new ones is a slow and difficult process. Striving for excellence means we have to take our time. If we are patient and keep working at it, we'll eventually achieve success.

FRIDAY:

Vince Lombardi, the great football coach, said, "We must pay a price for success. It's like anything worthwhile. It has a price. You have to pay the price to win and you have to pay the price to get to the point where success is possible. Most important, you must pay the price to stay there. Success is not a 'sometimes' thing. In other words, you don't do what is right once in a while, but all the time. Success is a habit. Winning is a habit."

CARING MESSAGE FOR WEEK 21:

Your actions speak louder than words!

MONDAY:

Actions speak louder than words. As Ben Franklin said, "Well done is better than well said."

TUESDAY:

A man of words and not of deeds
Is like a garden full of weeds.

—Mother Goose

WEDNESDAY:

Marie Curie, who won the Nobel Prizes in both physics and chemistry, said, "One never sees what has been done. One can only see what still needs to be done."

THURSDAY:

Rosa Parks is a woman who changed history by the simple act of refusing to give up her seat on a bus because of the color of her skin. It became the first step in a yearlong boycott of city buses that ended the hated laws separating the races. When you know something is right, don't be afraid to take that first step. You never know what good may later be accomplished from your action.

FRIDAY:

"We judge ourselves by what we feel capable of doing, while others judge us by what we have already done."

Henry Wadsworth Longfellow, 19th-century poet

Cooperate with a smile!

MONDAY:

Cooperation means people can work together for their mutual benefit. When we cooperate with others we combine our forces to try to reach common goals and to help each other. We can accomplish much more if we learn to work together, so let's join forces!

TUESDAY:

"We cannot live only for ourselves. A thousand fibers connect us with our fellow men; and among those fibers, our actions run as causes, and they come back to us as effects."

—*Herman Melville, author of* Moby-Dick

WEDNESDAY:

Eleanor Roosevelt told us that, "All things in human history have been arrived at slowly and through many compromises." So remember when we are working with others we may need to compromise to achieve our goals.

THURSDAY:

Our real worth in this life can only be measured by how much we have done for the benefit of others. The reason we need to cooperate is so that every person has the chance to feel special.

FRIDAY:

A Spanish proverb reminds us how much more we can accomplish when we work together: "Three men helping one another will do as much as six men alone."

CARING MESSAGE FOR WEEK 23:

Clear your mind of "can't!"

MONDAY:

"He that is good at making excuses, is seldom good at anything else."
—*Benjamin Franklin*

TUESDAY:

Thomas Edison once said, "Genius is one percent inspiration and ninety-nine percent perspiration." His great inventions weren't the result of one brilliant idea, but hundreds of experiments.

WEDNESDAY:

If you're having difficulty completing any kind of project, get some advice from someone. Many times an advisor can save us time by helping us avoid mistakes that have been made in the past. Use the experience of others.

THURSDAY:

Most people don't start out being successful at things they haven't tried before. Mastering any skill always involves a great deal of practice. Ask any athlete about how difficult it was to become good at a sport. Keep trying—and practice, practice, practice!

FRIDAY:

You can accomplish almost anything if you are really willing to work at it. Let's listen once again to Thomas Edison, who said, "Opportunity is missed by most people because it is dressed in overalls and looks like work."

CARING MESSAGE FOR WEEK 24:

If you don't stand for something, you may fall for anything!

MONDAY:

Courage requires us to speak out if we see something that we know is wrong. If we remain silent about it, people may think we agree with the wrongdoing.

TUESDAY:

Many times we forget to rely on our own common sense. Common sense is the ability to think before you act. If your common sense tells you something might not be a good choice, don't let someone convince you otherwise.

WEDNESDAY:

"Whoever is happy will make others happy too. He who has courage and faith will never perish in misery."

—Anne Frank

THURSDAY:

Eleanor Roosevelt was the First Lady during much of the Great Depression and World War II, and saw her husband die in the White House. She was a woman of courage who told us, "You gain strength, courage, and confidence by every experience in which you really stop to look fear in the face."

FRIDAY:

In her book *Dear Mrs. Parks*, Rosa Parks answers the letters of teens and gives them this advice: "It takes courage to grow up and reach your highest potential, not violence. We must respect and care for one another so that we can all live and be free."

Make new friends, but keep the old!

MONDAY:

"Each friend represents a world in us, a world possibly not born until they arrive, and it is only by this meeting that a new world is born."

—*Anaïs Nin*

TUESDAY:

Hubert Humphrey, a former U.S. Senator who ran for the presidency, said, "The greatest healing therapy is friendship and love." If you are having a hard time, turn to a friend for some healing power.

WEDNESDAY:

It's important to make new friends, for friends are the treasures of life. However, there is nothing quite like getting together with an old friend who knows you well. Is there an old friend you need to contact? Do it today.

THURSDAY:

George Washington reminded us of the importance of choosing friends carefully when he said, "It is better to be alone than to be in bad company." You will often be judged by the friends you keep so learn about the character of a person before you make him or her a friend.

FRIDAY:

Robert Louis Stevenson was a Scottish poet and novelist who became one of the world's greatest writers. He wrote of the true value of friendship: "A friend is a gift you give yourself."

CARING MESSAGE FOR WEEK 26:

Live a life of purpose!

MONDAY:

Being successful in life requires a plan. Some modern authors refer to it as a vision. It's what gives your life meaning. What is your plan for the future?

TUESDAY:

We know it's impossible to accomplish everything most of us would like to do in our lives, so we need to set priorities. What are the most important things to you? Make a list in order of importance. Start with a list of priorities that you need to accomplish in one day. You may be surprised at how this will keep you focused on your long-term goals.

WEDNESDAY:

Sometimes you need to make an adjustment and revise your goals. Don't let that discourage you from working toward your dreams.

THURSDAY:

An old Chinese proverb states, "A journey of a thousand miles begins with a single step." Even a small step in the right direction is progress toward your goal.

FRIDAY:

"You may be whatever you resolve to be. Determine to be something in the world and you will be something. 'I cannot' never accomplished anything. 'I will try' has wrought wonders."

—Sarah Hale, an American author

CARING MESSAGE FOR WEEK 27:

Study and the opportunities will come!

MONDAY:
"Be less curious about people and more curious about ideas."
—Marie Curie

TUESDAY:
Sir Francis Bacon, a great English philosopher and statesman, said, "Natural abilities are like natural plants that need pruning by studying!"

WEDNESDAY:
"Thinking is the hardest work there is, which is probably the reason why so few engage in it."
—Henry Ford

THURSDAY:
The greatest satisfaction in life comes when we know we have worked hard and lived up to our personal responsibilities. Your responsibility now is to your education.

FRIDAY:
Woodrow Wilson, 28th President of the U.S., said, "We should not only use the brains we have, but all that we can borrow." Try studying with a buddy this weekend.

CARING MESSAGE FOR WEEK 28:

Forgive honest mistakes!

MONDAY:

"Forgive and forget." Once we have forgiven someone for a mistake we should not keep reminding the person of that mistake.

TUESDAY:

Anwar Al-Sadat, the president of Egypt who gave his life working for peace in the Middle East, once said, "He who cannot change the very fabric of his thought will never ... make any progress."

WEDNESDAY:

An ancient Indian holy man, Dhammapadda, wrote, "There is no shark like hatred." Don't hold grudges against others.

THURSDAY:

Sometimes the hardest person to forgive is yourself! Admit your mistakes and try not to carry around a load of guilt, because that takes too much energy. Use the energy to forge ahead instead.

FRIDAY:

Only when you can forgive others and yourself will you really be at peace and feel deeply happy.

CARING MESSAGE FOR WEEK 29:

Nurture our environment!

MONDAY:

We have a responsibility to ourselves and others to respect all living things. If we don't, we are simply destroying our own future.

TUESDAY:

Look at the beautiful world around you! Notice its variations and how it changes. Do everything you can to preserve it.

WEDNESDAY:

Adopt the hallways of our school by picking up litter you see in the halls.

THURSDAY:

Theodore Roosevelt, our 26th President, was deeply concerned about conserving our natural resources. He said, "The nation behaves well if it treats the natural resources as assets which it must turn over to the next generation increased, and not impaired, in value."

FRIDAY:

Laura Ingalls Wilder, author of the Little House series, said, "I believe we would be happier to have a personal revolution in our individual lives and go back to simpler living and more direct thinking. It is the simple things in life that make living worthwhile ... such as love and duty, work and rest, and living close to nature." Spend some time enjoying the outdoors this weekend and be aware of the beauty of nature.

Be true to yourself!

MONDAY:

Before you make any important choices, be sure you have all the information you need. Be sure to seek the advice of those you trust and admire.

TUESDAY:

You must be willing to live with the consequences of your choices and learn from them.

WEDNESDAY:

"This above all, to thine own self be true,
And it must follow as the night the day
Thou canst not then be false to any man."

—William Shakespeare

THURSDAY:

The great scientist Galileo said, "You can't teach people anything. You can only help them discover it within themselves."

FRIDAY:

"Believe nothing, no matter where you read it, or who said it...unless it agrees with your own reason and your own common sense."

—Buddha, 6th Century B.C.

CARING MESSAGE FOR WEEK 31:

Hustle while you wait!

MONDAY:

"Lose no time," Benjamin Franklin said. "Be always prepared in something useful." When you are waiting in line or for an appointment, read a book or get some studying done.

TUESDAY:

Opportunities don't just happen to us—we can create them if we are willing to work and accept responsibility.

WEDNESDAY:

The Greek philosopher Socrates, who died for his ideas, said, "If a man would move the world, first he must move himself."

THURSDAY:

Thomas Edison said, "If we did all of the things we were capable of doing, we would literally astound ourselves." What could you be doing instead of watching TV?

FRIDAY:

Sometimes when we think something will be difficult, we tend to exaggerate its difficulty, making it seem much harder than it is. Start by taking small steps and you may be amazed how quickly the job you thought you couldn't accomplish will get done.

Be a team player!

MONDAY:

Encourage teamwork in others and be a good team player yourself. Congratulate other members of your team for a strong effort. Don't gloat over your own successes.

TUESDAY:

A team is not just a sports team. Think of your family, class, or community as a team. The same principles of success apply to them, so learn to work with others on many teams.

WEDNESDAY:

Set realistic personal goals for yourself and share them with your teammates. Work together to establish some team goals.

THURSDAY:

A Native American leader, Chief Seattle, said, "Man does not weave this web of life. He is merely a strand of it. Whatever he does to the web, he does to himself." Let's remember how much we need other people.

FRIDAY:

You will have bad games. Admit your mistakes honestly. Look to your teammates for advice and support. Be sympathetic when other members of the team are not quite up to par.

CARING MESSAGE FOR WEEK 33:

Always do right!

MONDAY:

"You never have to apologize for doing the right thing."

—Ginny Turner, author

TUESDAY:

"Fear less, hope more;
Whine less, breathe more;
Talk less, say more;
Hate less, love more;
And all good things are yours."

—Anonymous

WEDNESDAY:

An 18th Century monk said, "Living the truth in your heart without compromise brings kindness into the world."

THURSDAY:

You will influence many people by showing that you have the courage to do the right thing. Your example will help others do the right thing.

FRIDAY:

Rosa Parks tells us, "I learned from my grandmother and mother that one should always respect oneself and live right. This is how you gain the respect of others." So if we want respect, we must earn it.

CARING MESSAGE FOR WEEK 34:

Challenge your mind!

MONDAY:

An education doesn't depend on how much you commit to memory. It's more important to be a good problem solver and to know where to find the needed information. Becoming a good problem solver takes practice, but it will help you all your life.

TUESDAY:

Challenging your mind is hard work. The Greek philosopher Aristotle said, "The educated differ from the uneducated as much as the living from the dead."

WEDNESDAY:

If you're going to be an educated person, you must have the desire to learn. If you don't want something to happen you will sabotage your own chance for success.

THURSDAY:

Learning is a process. It involves training and practice just like any other skill. So set frustration aside and go forward one step at a time.

FRIDAY:

An ancient Chinese proverb states, "The teacher can lead the student to the door, but the acquisition of learning is the responsibility of the student." Concentrate and think in your classes so you won't miss opportunities to learn.

Make someone feel accepted!

MONDAY:

Never underestimate the power of a smile. Even if you don't know some-one, it doesn't hurt to smile, and it can brighten someone's day. Your teachers love to see you smiling.

TUESDAY:

Empathy is the ability to sense and understand the feelings of another person. It is not the same thing as feeling sorry for someone, because sometimes when we do that we are looking down on that person. Try to work on your ability to feel empathy: nothing makes another person feel better than to know someone else understands.

WEDNESDAY:

Think about this poem by Edwin Markham:

He drew a circle that shut me out-
Heretic, rebel, a thing to flout.
But Love and I had the wit to win,
We drew a circle and let him in!

THURSDAY:

"If you treat an individual ... as if he were what he ought to be and could be, he will become what he ought to be and could be."

—Goethe

FRIDAY:

Sometimes when a person faces a life-threatening situation they have regrets or wish they could tell someone how much they really mean to them. Find some way to show your love to someone important in your life—it could be as simple as asking, "How did things go for you today?" and listening carefully to the answer.

CARING MESSAGE FOR WEEK 36:

You can never be too kind!

MONDAY:

The great Greek philosopher Plato said, "Be kind, for everyone you meet is fighting a harder battle!" You can never tell what difficulties another person is facing, and your kind word might make all the difference.

TUESDAY:

"Flowers leave part of their fragrance in the hands that bestow them."
—*Chinese proverb*

WEDNESDAY:

"Kindness and generosity are the richest gifts you can give someone, especially when they are unexpected."
—*Ginny Turner, author*

THURSDAY:

Most trouble between people, begins when someone puts down another person, and hurt feelings lead to bad behavior. Be different. Let your little acts of kindness lift people up.

FRIDAY:

"I expect to pass the world but once,
any good therefore that I can do,
or any kindness that I can show
to any fellow creature, let me do it now.
let me not deter or neglect it,
for I shall not pass this way again."

—*Unknown*

CARING MESSAGE FOR WEEK 37:

Speak the truth!

MONDAY:

Remember the oath witnesses say in court: "I promise to tell the truth, the whole truth, and nothing but the truth." As Ben Franklin pointed out, "Half the truth is often a great lie."

TUESDAY:

"You must speak straight so that your words may go like sunlight to our hearts."

—*Cochise, leader of the Apache Nation*

WEDNESDAY:

"So live your life that your autograph will be wanted instead of your fingerprints."

—*Unknown*

THURSDAY:

Aesop said, "Every truth has two sides. It is well to look at both, before we commit ourselves to either." So try to get both sides of the story before making any decisions.

FRIDAY:

For our final message about truth, let us listen to Martin Luther King Jr.:

"I have tried to be honest. To be honest is to confront the truth however unpleasant and inconvenient the truth may be. I believe we must expose and face it if we are to achieve a better quality of American life."

CARING MESSAGE FOR WEEK 38:

Learn to keep your cool!

MONDAY:

Self-discipline is the ability to do what you should do and keep from doing what you should not do. You have complete freedom to be in charge of yourself. Only when you achieve self-discipline can you really have power over your life.

TUESDAY:

Self-restraint is a sign of emotional maturity. It helps us think a moment before we act or speak. That moment can mean the difference between peace and serious consequences.

WEDNESDAY:

Eleanor Roosevelt was not pretty and was often criticized for her appearance, which might have made her feel constantly put down. Instead, she said, "No one can make you feel inferior without your consent."

THURSDAY:

If you allow someone to make you angry, you have given that person power over you. That person now has control over your emotions.

FRIDAY:

Again let us learn a lesson by listening to the words of Martin Luther King Jr., who preached about the importance of non-violence. "You must be willing to suffer the anger of the opponent, and yet not return anger. No matter how emotional your opponents are, you must remain calm."

The future never comes all at once!

MONDAY:

English poet Elizabeth Barrett Browning wrote, "Light tomorrow with today." Instead of thinking about your future as something that will occur much later, consider that your future will be a result of what you do today.

TUESDAY:

General George S. Patton, who commanded American troops in World War II, said, "Success is how high you bounce when you hit bottom." So don't be afraid to fail—just keep trying!

WEDNESDAY:

We must learn to be patient if we want to be successful in life. A Chinese proverb tells us: "Patience is power. With time and patience the mulberry leaf becomes silk."

THURSDAY:

The kind of student you are today will affect the kind of future you have. If your salary depended on how hard you're working in school this year, how would you measure up?

FRIDAY:

Theodore Roosevelt, our 26th President, advised, "Keep your eyes on the stars and your feet on the ground." It's important to have dreams, but we have to work for them. Learn from past mistakes and make sure you have all of the facts before you make decisions.

CARING MESSAGE FOR WEEK 40:

Be a person of character!

MONDAY:
Listen today to the words of Horace Greeley: "Fame is vapor, popularity an accident, riches take wings. Only one thing endures, and that is character."

TUESDAY:
"Good character, like good soup, is usually homemade."

—Unknown

WEDNESDAY:
John Adams, the second President of the U.S., wrote the following in a letter to his son John Quincy Adams: "You will remember that All the End of study is to make you a good Man and a useful Citizen."

THURSDAY:
"Parents can only give good advice or put [their children] on the right paths, but the final forming of a person's character lies in their own hands."

—Anne Frank

FRIDAY:
Your character is who you are when no one is looking.

Part II:
Special Occasions

Labor Day

Columbus Day

Election Day

Veterans Day

Thanksgiving Day

Pearl Harbor

Martin Luther King Jr. Day

Abraham Lincoln's Birthday

George Washington's Birthday

Earth Day

Memorial Day

Flag Day

Drug-Free Week

LABOR DAY

The first Labor Day was celebrated on Sept. 5, 1882, when ten thousand workers held a parade in New York City to honor all of our nation's workers. This parade was staged by the Knights of Labor, and many of the marchers knew they could lose their jobs for participating.

In 1894, Congress passed a bill making the first Monday in September a national holiday. On this day remember that the prosperity of our nation depends on work done by people in all kinds of occupations. It is important that we think about the value of hard work and remember that it doesn't matter what we do as long as we do it well.

COLUMBUS DAY

On October 12, 1492, Christopher Columbus, sailing under the flag of Spain, knelt in thanksgiving on the beaches of an island in the Bahamas that he named San Salvador. His goal had been to find a shorter sea route to the Indies. He did not realize that he had landed near a continent that was unknown to Europeans—North America. He later made three other voyages to nearby islands. He and his men encountered native peoples who exchanged ideas and products with them. Columbus was an excellent seaman who had great courage, and his voyages led to a lasting contact between Europe and America.

ELECTION DAY

Be proud to be an American and to live in a democratic country where we can make choices and voice our opinions. Voting is one of our most important rights—it allows us to choose the people who represent us in all levels of government—and yet many Americans do not take advantage of this right. Throughout our history, women, African Americans, and other groups have fought hard to win the right to vote. Encourage others to exercise this important right and to make wise choices about the future leadership of our country.

VETERANS DAY

Veterans Day was originally called Armistice Day because it is celebrated to commemorate that day near the end of World War I when the nations fighting in the war agreed to "lay down their weapons," and work for peace. They agreed to do this on the eleventh hour, of the eleventh day, in the eleventh month of 1918.

In 1921, an American soldier—his name "known but to God"—was buried in Arlington National Cemetery at the Tomb of the Unknown Soldier. Similar ceremonies also took place in England and France. If World War I had been "the War to end all wars," we might still call this day Armistice Day, but unfortunately the fighting in World War II shattered this dream.

In 1954, President Eisenhower signed the bill proclaiming November 11 as Veterans Day. It is a day to remember all of the men and women who have served our country in the armed services. We hope they will be in your thoughts as we celebrate the holiday. If you have the opportunity, we hope that you, personally, will thank a veteran for serving our country and protecting our freedom.

> **"Let us solemnly remember the sacrifices of all those who fought so valiantly, on the seas, in the air, and on foreign shores, to preserve our heritage of freedom, and let us reconsecrate ourselves to the task of promoting an enduring peace so that their efforts shall not have been in vain."**
>
> Dwight D. Eisenhower
> Presidential Proclamation 3071
> Veterans Day, 1954

THANKSGIVING DAY

By the autumn of 1621, the Pilgrims had endured the first winter and had reaped their first harvest. Governor William Bradford called for a thanksgiving feast to be celebrated with Chief Massasoit and his people, who had taught the Pilgrims how to plant corn and had shown them other skills needed to survive in the wilderness. Some historians believe the party may have lasted for several days.

In New England, people began to celebrate this feast every year. However, Thanksgiving Day did not become a national celebration until 1863, when Sarah Hale, editor of a ladies' book, convinced Abraham Lincoln to make it a holiday. As you celebrate this feast with family and friends, be thankful for all of your blessings, and remember those two groups of people from different cultures who worked together and thus were able to survive.

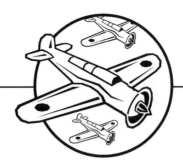

PEARL HARBOR
December 7

President Franklin D. Roosevelt said that December 7, 1941 was "a date which will live in infamy." He was asking Congress to declare war on Japan because of their surprise bombing at Pearl Harbor, Hawaii, at the same time they were negotiating through diplomats in Washington, D.C. On this Sunday morning, the city of Honolulu was not quite awake, and the bulk of the U.S. Pacific fleet was anchored at the naval base at Pearl Harbor. In less than two hours, the Japanese attack sunk or severely damaged seven battleships, demolished one hundred and forty planes and damaged eighty more, caused the loss of 2330 American lives, and wounded another 1145 sailors, marines, and civilians. This brought the United States into World War II, and today as we think about the devastation of war, let us remember all of the men and women who served our country at that tragic time.

MARTIN LUTHER KING JR. DAY

January 15, 1929 was the birth date of Martin Luther King Jr., who followed in his father's footsteps and became a Baptist minister in Atlanta. In 1955, he became actively involved in the Civil Rights Movement, which sought to gain social and political rights for black Americans. He believed in the use of nonviolent methods to gain social and political rights, and his nonviolent actions included projects such as the famous Montgomery bus boycott, marches, sit-ins at restaurants that discriminated against African Americans, and, of course, speeches. His most famous speech, titled, "I have a dream," was delivered on the steps of the Lincoln Memorial during the massive march on Washington, D. C. in 1963.

He paid a very heavy price for his efforts to gain for blacks the same rights that white Americans had. His house was bombed; he was jailed, stoned, and beaten; and after many threats on his own life, he was assassinated in April 1968. Let us remember him today and in his memory work to find peace in our own lives.

ABRAHAM LINCOLN'S BIRTHDAY – February 12

Abraham Lincoln was born on February 12, 1809, in a log cabin in the backwoods of Kentucky. He was very poor, his mother died when he was very young, and he had little formal schooling, although he loved learning. He became a lawyer and served in the House of Representatives, but lost elections for the Senate. In 1860, however, he became the first Republican President of the United States.

The sophisticated people in Washington made fun of him and called him a "baboon." He was devastated by the beginning of the Civil War and promised to "preserve, protect, and defend" the Union. While he did not believe in slavery himself, his main goal was always to keep the country together. Nevertheless, in an effort to end the war more quickly, Lincoln issued the famous Emancipation Proclamation, which officially freed the first slaves.

Just five days after the Civil War came to an end, he was assassinated. He had made plans for peace and begged people not to seek revenge for the hardships and heartbreak of the war. He called for us "...to do all which may achieve...a just and lasting peace among ourselves and with all nations."

GEORGE WASHINGTON'S BIRTHDAY – February 22

George Washington was born February 22, 1732 on a Virginia plantation. He was a surveyor and a landowner, and gained a reputation as a commander in the French and Indian War. At the age of 43, he arrived in Massachusetts and used his military genius to command the Continental Army, which eventually defeated the British in the American Revolution.

After the War, his influence in getting the U. S. Constitution adopted led the state electors to vote unanimously for him to become our first President. He longed to retire to his estate at Mount Vernon but felt the compelling need to serve his country once again, and served as President for eight years. In 1798, he was actually called upon once again to command U. S. troops against France, but fortunately, the disputes were settled without war.

Let us remember him as a great leader who put aside his own desires and comforts to continually serve his country. When he died, he was probably best remembered in a tribute by Henry Lee, who had served under Washington in the cavalry. He described his former commander as "First in war, first in peace, and first in the hearts of his countrymen."

EARTH DAY
April 22

On April 22, 1970, hundreds of thousands of Americans took part in the first celebration of Earth Day. Activists held demonstrations, rallies, and teach-ins to show their deep concerns about pollution and the destruction of the environment. They tried to create an awareness of the need for a campaign to protect our environment for future generations. The movement gained support from many Americans who began to see pollution as a threat to the health of their families. Congress passed the National Environmental Policy Act, which was soon followed by the Clean Air and Clean Water Acts. In 1970, the Environmental Protection Agency was also formed to set and enforce pollution standards, conduct research, and assist state and local governments in dealing with environmental concerns.

As we celebrate Earth Day, let us remember to do our part to show respect for the environment and think about how individuals can work together to bring about positive changes in our world. Those early activists certainly were effective in bringing about changes that have benefited all Americans. Let's continue their efforts.

MEMORIAL DAY

The origins of Memorial Day actually go back to the 1860's. A volunteer, Elizabeth Rutherford Ellis, had taken care of the sick and dying in the South during the Civil War. She also visited the graves of the soldiers and encouraged the Southern states to establish a holiday to honor them after the war.

Shortly after the war, Mary Logan was visiting the South and was impressed when she saw how people had decorated the graves of the soldiers. Her husband was a general in the Union army and she encouraged him to get Congress to pass a law for a national holiday. On May 30, 1868 Americans celebrated the first Decoration Day. It received this name because the people decorated the graves of those who had died in war.

Since World War I, this day, now called Memorial Day, has been set aside to honor all of the men and women who died serving our country in any war. So let us remember these brave men and women who gave the ultimate sacrifice of life in order to assure our continued freedom.

FLAG DAY
June 14

Flag Day is celebrated on June 14 in memory of the day in 1777 when the Continental Congress adopted the Stars and Stripes as the official flag of the United States. In 1877, the government requested that the flag be flown over all public buildings in honor of its 100th anniversary. President Harry S. Truman officially recognized June 14 as Flag Day. As you say the pledge of allegiance, and see the flag displayed today, be proud to be an American and happy that we live in a free country. Perhaps you can also display an American flag at home.

CARING MESSAGE FOR
"DRUG FREE WEEK":

Be proud to be drug free!

MONDAY:

This is the beginning of "drug free" week in our community.

Have the courage to make the right choice and be drug free!

TUESDAY:

By saying "No" to drugs you can say "Yes" to life. Remember the words of Leo Tolstoy: "Our body is a machine for living. It is organized for that; it is its nature. Let life go on in it."

Don't pollute your body with harmful substances.

WEDNESDAY:

Do your part to create a drug free world! Display your red ribbon properly and wear it proudly today!*

THURSDAY:

Friends respect our good choices and may be led by our good example. Make the right decision to have a healthy mind, body, and spirit. Encourage others to do the same.

FRIDAY:

There is a very powerful saying that states, "Don't follow the crowd— follow your conscience!" Be a strong enough person to ignore negative peer pressure.

In many schools students are given special red ribbons, often with slogans, to wear on this day. It is a nice idea to provide the ribbons for all of the adults, including the bus drivers. Many communities also hold public events in front of schools and town buildings, and have students make banners that are proudly displayed in the community during the week.

NOTES

NOTES

NOTES

NOTES

NOTES

NOTES

Character Development Publishing Order Form

TITLE	PRICE	QTY.	$ TOTAL
Advisor/Advisee Character Education LESSONS FOR TEACHERS AND COUNSELORS Sarah Sadlow, 8x11, 120 pages, softcover, ISBN 0-9653163-7-8	$24.95		
America's Pride & Promise Teacher's Kit RELEARNING THE MEANING OF THE PLEDGE OF ALLEGIANCE Rhonda Adams, CD, Sheet Music, Teacher's Guide, Classroom Poster, ISBN 1-892056-16-x	$39.95		
Building Character Schoolwide BUILDING A CARING COMMUNITY IN YOUR SCHOOL R. Bernardo, L. Frye, D. Smith, G. Foy, 8x11, 153 pages, softcover, ISBN 1-892056-10-0	$18.00		
Caring Messages 40 WEEKS OF DAILY DISCUSSION IDEAS ON CHARACTER Sharon L. Banas, 8x11", 56 loose leaf pages, ISBN 1-892056-12-7	$14.95		
Character Education Through Story LESSONS FROM MULTI-CULTURAL LITERATURE K-6 Dr. Joseph Hester, Paul Coble Fellow, 8x11, 488 pages, softcover, ISBN 1-892056-20-8	$39.95		
Cultivating Heart and Character EDUCATING FOR LIFE'S MOST ESSENTIAL GOALS T. Devine, J. H. Seuk, A. Wilson, 6x9, 486 pages, softcover, ISBN 1-892056-15-1	$22.95		
Developing Character for Classroom Success STRATEGIES FOR SECONDARY STUDENTS Charlie Abourjilie, 6x9, 96 pages, softcover, ISBN 1-892056-07-0	$12.00		
Developing Character in Students, 2nd Edition A PRIMER FOR TEACHERS, PARENTS, AND COMMUNITIES Dr. Philip Fitch Vincent, 6x9, 174 pages, softcover, ISBN 1-892-05604-6	$19.95		
Elementary School Guide to Character Education Steve Dixon, 6x9, 120 pages, softcover, ISBN 1-892056-17-8	$15.95		
A Gift of Character: The Chattanooga Story 6x9, 220 pages, softcover, ISBN 1-892056-16-x	$15.95		
Hey, Mr. McRay ANSWERING TEENS ON ISSUES OF JUDGMENT AND CHARACTER Dr. Michael R. McGough, 6x9, 200 pages, softcover, ISBN 1-892056-14-3	$14.95		
Lessons From the Rocking Chair TIMELESS STORIES FOR TEACHING CHARACTER Deb Austin Brown, 6x9, 70 pages, softcover, ISBN 0-9653163-3-5	$8.95		
Life's Greatest Lessons 20 THINGS I WANT MY KIDS TO KNOW Hal Urban, 6x9, 162 pages, softcover, ISBN 0-9659684-4-8	$14.95		
Operating Manual for Character Education Programs 3-ring binder, 9x12, 327 pages, ISBN 1-892056-13-5	$79.95		
Parents, Kids & Character 21 STRATEGIES TO HELP YOUR CHILDREN DEVELOP GOOD CHARACTER Dr. Helen LeGette, 6x9, 180 pages, softcover, ISBN 1-892056-01-1	$15.95		
Promising Practices in Character Education, Vol. 1 NINE SUCCESS STORIES FROM ACROSS THE COUNTRY Edited by Dr. Philip Fitch Vincent, 6x9, 112 pages, softcover, ISBN 0-9653163-0-0	$12.00		
Promising Practices in Character Education, Vol. 2 12 MORE SUCCESS STORIES FROM ACROSS THE COUNTRY Foreword by Dr. Philip Fitch Vincent, 6x9, 148 pages, softcover, ISBN 1-892056-02-4-x	$14.00		
Rules & Procedures THE FIRST STEP TOWARD SCHOOL CIVILITY, 2nd EDITION Dr. Philip Fitch Vincent, 6x9, 96 pages, softcover, ISBN 1-892056-06-2	$14.00		
Rules & Procedures on Video THE FIRST STEP TOWARD SCHOOL CIVILITY (VIDEO) Dr. Philip Fitch Vincent, VHS, 44 minutes, ISBN 1-892056-03-8	$59.95		
BEST SELLER! **Teaching Character...It's Elementary** 36 WEEKS OF DAILY LESSONS FOR GRADES K-5 S. A. Broome, N. W. Henley, 8x11, 232 pages, softcover, ISBN 1-892056-08-9	$27.95		
Teaching Character: Parent's Idea Book A. C. Dotson and K. D. Wisont, 8x11, 84 pages, softcover, ISBN 0-9653163-5-1	$12.00		
BEST SELLER! **Teaching Character: Teacher's Idea Book** A. C. Dotson and K. D. Wisont, 8x11, 160 pages, softcover, ISBN 0-9653163-4-3	$24.00		

CHARACTER DEVELOPMENT PUBLISHING

Pay with credit card or make checks payable to:
Character Development Publishing
PO Box 9211, Chapel Hill, NC 27515
(919) 967-2110, (919) 967-2139 fax
Respect96@aol.com
www.CharacterEducation.com

(North Carolina residents add 6.5%)

6% SHIPPING WITH A $4 MINIMUM

Subtotal	
Sales tax	
Shipping	
TOTAL	

SHIP TO:
Name _____
Organization _____ Title _____
Address _____
City _____ State: _____ Zip: _____
Phone: ( ) _____ Fax: ( ) _____ PO#: _____
Visa or MasterCard number: _____ Exp. Date: _____
Signature: _____

FAX your order
(919) 967-2139,
call us
(919) 967-2110,
or order from our website:
www.CharacterEducation.com